NICOLE JOHNSON

AuthorHouse™ LLC
1663 Liberty Drive
Bloomington, IN 47403
www.authorhouse.com
Phone: 1-800-839-8640

Published by AuthorHouse 03/18/2014

ISBN: 978-1-4918-6984-0 (sc)
978-1-4918-6983-3 (e)

Dedication

Thank you to everyone who has been with me this far.

I would like to dedicate this to a few special people,

You know who you are.

"Her world inside out"

Music is my life but

Poetry is my story.

Put them both together and you could really get to know me.

Judge me if you want to based only on what you've heard;

or take the time to listen to a story you misunderstood.

No one here knows me better than I know myself.

Here it is my story

"Her world inside out."

S.T.R.E.N.G.T.H.

Standing. Tall. Reminding. Everyone. Nothing. Gets. Too. Hard

Strength

When life is hard do not give up
show the world that you are tough.
When things get bad and don't go your way
remember there will be another day
When you can't find the strength inside
remember strength is what keeps you alive.

Hold Tight

Don't leave someone you love for someone you like.
If it's not working out just hold on tight.
Don't be annoyed by people in life that are trying to keep you
From making the biggest mistake of your life.
If you find your heart is in so much pain you should
Probably know you made yourself that way.

Pick Your Poison

I'm no longer going to look at you I'm looking past you.
You've picked your poison now deal with the consequences of your actions.
Do not expect me to be the same person who I was because she's no longer here.
You can't just put a rain check on love.
In my eyes you do not seem happy but I shouldn't care because you turned your back to me.
From here on out I am doing things my way and when your world comes
tumbling down remember you could've had me.
When I can see the sunshine again and all you can see are gray clouds; that's when
my life will be back on track because you're feeling the same pain I had for you in the past.

No strength or Courage

I don't know if I'll ever have the courage to tell anyone how I feel
It's amazing how just that one person can break you down into tears.
I'm trying hard to be strong for myself but I can't tell you
How impossible it is
When everything you believed was true
Really turned out to be just a tale.
Right now I just want you to know that you took everything that I had
My strength, my courage, and my reason for living
because everything you said you felt wasn't real.

Find yourself

With every breath taken, with words never said,
is one more emotion that you chose and you held.
With so little time being unsure of yourself is another
Precious moment wasted that could've been spent on something else.
With no hope left and all faith gone, you look in the mirror and wonder who you've become.
With strength and courage that's somewhere hidden inside,
You will find yourself again and you will no longer have to hide.

Legacy

What's your name?
Where are you from?
Who is the person you want to become?
Make your mark and don't regret a thing;
Everything you do will be worth it one day just wait and see.
What you want the world to remember about you
Will happen if you give it a try.
Nothing is worse than letting your dreams fade away to die.
Your legacy and your purpose here will mean the world to someone one day,
But you can't let anyone in this world hold you back today.

Fix the broken pieces

Take my hand
don't let go
hold it tight
to prepare me for the worse.
Say it slow
not too fast
Let each word sit awhile
so it doesn't sound bad.
Pain cuts deep
but memories last
and because of them I will never forget the past.
Simple words used only to heal
will mend my heart for the following years.

P.o.s.s.i.b.l.e

Power. Of. Simple. Situations. Initiated. By. Life's. Ecstasy

Never Impossible

Doing the impossible is easier than it sounds
if you take all of your problems and face them head on.
When you say that you can't you suddenly become a failure
And at that point that's what everyone will remember.
If you tell yourself that you can do it and nothing will stand in your way,
That one thing that you thought was impossible will be possible again.

Trust

How can I see when the road ahead is so cloudy?
I reach for a hand in hopes that someone will guide me.
How can I trust the person who guides me?
By trusting the person who is willing to find me.

Perfectly Imperfect

I'm not the prettiest girl in the world nor do I want to be.
I may not have the most perfect skin or a gorgeous "killer body."
Movie star, runway model, showstopper? No way!
Pretty clothes, perfect hair? No, but maybe I will one day.
Would this be the life that I would choose? A life of luxury.
Yes if only I could get everyone to except me for being me.
I would love to stop being judged based on the person that I am;
But if I ever got the chance I'd prove to everyone that I can.
I can be a role model, a leader, or a friend. I could be your inspiration
Not a picture perfect person.
I am perfectly imperfect and what exactly does that mean;
It means that I'm not perfect but I am happy with just being me.

G.O.D.

Guiding. Our. Direction

Nicole's Prayer

As I drop my head and fold my hands all I want is for you to hear me out.
I want you to know where I stand in this world and what my life is really all about.
There is an empty spot where my heart should be and a person who I feel should fill it.
There's a voice that tells me every day to move on with my life, he's not worth it.
I cover my ears to block everyone out, I listen for your voice but I never hear it.
I want you to tell me things will fall into place and everything I have always waited
For was worth it.

Gods Promise

The way I look at the world may be completely different than you do.
When I wake up each and every morning I see things in a completely different view.
Some people take their lives for granted and some just do not have a choice,
to deal with the battles and struggles in their lives
because they were not as fortunate as the rest.
They were given a life to grow up in that was much harder than other people they knew.
People would always look down on you because of some kind of secret that they knew.
When there are people like this in the world you think there is nothing that you can do.
So you sit in the corner with your hands on your head, crying asking God why did this have to be you.
He then says to you "my child please wipe your tears I promise your life will get better.
Continue to hold your head up high and remember that I will never fail you."

God's hands

God's hands

gave me

strength today

to live my life

in my own way

I'm Sorry

I'm sorry for everything that I have done
I'm sorry that you were right and I was wrong.
I'm sorry I didn't listen when you said to follow your heart.
I'm sorry I'm the one standing here all torn apart.
I'm sorry I never paid attention to the signs that you've sent me;
Now I'm asking dear God to please,
Please forgive me.

My savior

Each and every single day God takes my hand to lead the way.
He always seems to be by my side when no one else can hear my cries.
He lets me know that when I am weak he has the power to strengthen me.
He never wants to let us down he's listening even if it seems like he's not around.
If no one else understands your pain learn to accept your loss and you will
eventually gain.

Guardian Angel

One Guardian angel sits next to me with
Two reasons why he'll never leave;
Always around to protect me from the bad
And will always be here for me when I am sad.
Three wise people stand before me with
Four different things I will always carry with me:
A key for closure
Two doves for love
A cross for peace
And a four leaf clover for luck
Five secrets kept
Six promises made
One un-loyal person trying to put me in pain.
But I am stronger now than ever before and
It's all because of my guardian angel from above.

P.A.I.N

(Pretending. Advice. Isn't. Needed.)

You pretend advice isn't needed
But you know it's the only cure.
A cure given by someone
who you know really cares.

Emotions

Why do we hide our emotions inside?
If we cry we cry it's because were hurting inside.
Why do we get so mad with no one to blame?
We scream we complain but inside you feel the same.
Why do we care what people say?
We're only human and it's okay to feel this way.

Follow his path

Put a smile on your face
One day you will be okay.
Be around people who make you laugh
Not the ones who make you sad.
Love yourself before anyone else
Your heart cannot take too much more stress.
Find a dream and go for it.
You can't let people stand in the way of his guidance.
When you find the path that he has drawn
Follow it and you won't lead to harm.

Loved and Lost

I've lost more than I've loved but I didn't see
That losing way too much had the power to weaken me.
I've loved very little because I knew that when I did
The person who I loved would turn their back to me in the end.

Thinking about you

Behind every smile there is a little pain
With every new day it slowly fades away.
If the future brings us together
or keeps us far apart
You will always be the person in my deepest thoughts.
You're on my mind, I swear 24/7
You're my last thought at night
and the first one at sunrise.
You meant the world to me
But I guess now that doesn't mean a thing.
I think about you every single day
And it hurts knowing that you never think about me.

What hurts the most

You left without ever saying goodbye,
and never gave a reason why.
You had me floating on cloud 9
so I fell hard for you and all of the lies.
I don't know how to deal with it,
I've tried to focus energy on something else
so the pain in my heart was not what I felt.
It's not fair that I still think about you.
As much as I love the memories I want to go on living life like you do.
Just in case you didn't know this right here
is what hurts the most.

Nothing without you

Everything that I could possibly want
Is right within my reach,
But I would trade all that I have
for a chance at you and me.
Take the pearls off of my neck,
the diamonds off my finger,
and the clothes off my back.
All of it means nothing to me,
they can have it all.
It does not mean a thing to me
If I don't have you by my side.

Appreciate life

Waiting for something that will never be yours
Is harder than it seems.
You spend most of the day and your entire night
Hoping that maybe one day it will be.
For now take the time to appreciate what you have
And don't dwell on something that's not.
Your life will be much easier than it is
And I can definitely promise you that.

Pain, pain go away

I need to know if you can fix a broken heart if it was never whole to begin with.
The guy she wants is with someone else and their final moments together are approaching.
She wanted to let him know she had feelings for him but never got the courage to say.
She was scared to try and terrified of being turned down that she couldn't stomach the pain.
She knew that even if he liked her back he'd be too afraid to express it.
He never once considered his own feeling because he was afraid that his clique would harass him.
If I could pick one day in time I would pick the day before I ever met him.

Best friend; worst enemy

You take all their drama and breathe it in;
It will always be there stay away if you can.
Look ahead in the world and stand up tall
To everyone who has been doing you wrong.
Picture the perfect moment when everyone's
On your side and you are with your perfect guy
Imagine that the world looks at you like you're no different than them.
It might be surprising to know that you do exist.
Existing in this world means making a difference in this world
Doing it with or without the help of your friends.

Love Hurts

It will never kill you to tell them exactly how you feel.
Hours, days, and months pass by and they still have no idea.
Pressure in your chest goes up and your heart begins to race.
It's the feeling you get when they walk by and you act like you have nothing to say.
Take a deep breath and breathe in surrounding air. Be brave and courageous
God gave you hope to live with today.
Open your mouth, look into their eyes and tell them exactly what is on your mind.
Smile to them gently they'll smile back too and you may just find out that they
Felt the same way about you.
Love hurts and it's a pain we don't want to go through.

He said

To satisfy what you wanted I sacrificed my heart
You told me things I wanted to hear
and I believed things would be alright.
You told me you wouldn't hurt me.
You said you're not playing with my head.
You said that you really liked me;
but deep inside you never did.

Dreams not reality

I hate the facts that dreams never come true but the nightmares we have frequently do. The climax of your dreams feel so real and true then you're forced to wake up and deal with the same old you. The pictures you dreamed of, the sounds, and the motions were only in your dreams to teach you a lesson. If I could really wish upon a shooting star, I would wish that the dream cloud traveled far off into the sky. It will prevent me from dreaming big and getting my hopes too high because you can only wish upon a shooting star one time while it's in the sky.

Butterflies

The easiest things are always the hardest to say
Because no one knows if you feel the same way.
The hardest steps in life cannot be done in a day.
It takes time for all of your butterflies to fly away.
Why is it so simple for people to walk away?
Because by taking that path means not falling hard on your face.

I Promise

I promise I won't take your heart and hurt it like she did.
I promise if you want me to I'll leave you alone forever
Because I care.
I promise if things between us get really bad I'll do my best to work it out.
But I promise you that nothing will be as bad as
Shutting each other out.
My final promise to you is that everything will be okay
If you give me a chance.
I promise that the person I am today is the same person
I'll be in the end.

Part 1.

Crystal Clear

Okay I get it you have finally painted the picture crystal clear.
You no longer have to worry about me
I'll leave you alone forever I swear.
Please do not suddenly have a change of heart when I'm with somebody else.
I'm trying my hardest to get back on track but your acting like everything is alright.
All I ask is that you please promise me this one thing.
When your heart is healed don't push the next girl away
Like you did to me.

Part 2.

Waterfalls

My heart feels like someone ripped away the bandage
That was keeping it together.
I need to be strong now I know things will get better
And this pain will not last forever.
The rushing waters running down my face feel like a never ending stream
Of sorrow
Hating myself because the situations out of my control
And I know the only person to blame is myself.
I was often told never to change for anyone
And never let anyone judge you but God.
I will stick to this advice till the day that I die
And ignore the people who's not by my side
I don't know when I'll be happy again or when the
Waterfalls will stop falling from my eyes.

The Girl

She's got love in her heart and tears in her eyes
from way too many things.
She's got a smile that's pretty
and a voice that's tiny
because she's afraid to speak.
She's got family to love and no one else
because she is who she is.
She's got a pillow she lays on every night
that's drowned in her tears.
She's got talents unnoticed and wishes unspoken
because she's afraid to try
but most of all she's got a future
and that's where everything lies.
She may not be the most perfect girl
but that's who I am inside.

Mind Control

If my mind is what controls my heart
Then why do they disagree on who is right?
One is telling me to just face the facts
He is gone and he isn't coming back.
The other side is slowly breaking apart but it stays strong
Because it hasn't lost hope yet.
It knows that letting go is the only way out
But doing so means tearing me apart.
My mind is screaming to forget it all but
My heart overpowers it making it a tough call.
I take a step back and put reality aside
I contemplate all of the choices that I have.
I want to listen to my heart but it's hard
Knowing that my mind is the one who's right.

She is me

She is sad but she won't show it
She wants to cry and let the whole world know it.
She wants to beg and she wants to plead
But that's not the person who she wants to be.
She is crazy about him but she can't tell him
She needs to find the strength in herself to understand him.
She is confused and doesn't know what to do
He is hurting her more than he even knew.
She'll wipe the tears falling from her eyes and
Put on a smile that hides it all
Then I'll stand up nice and tall
And pretend like it's not killing me at all.

I.N.S.P.I.R.E.D.

Imagine. Never. Stopping. People. In. Realizing. Every. Dream.

Live each day to the fullest

Never be afraid to go for what you have always dreamed of.
Don't ever let yourself fall short of something you're so close to achieving.
Let each day be another one that you're grateful to be a part of;
A day that you can look to the sky and thank God again for the honor.

Truth is

Truth is you were someone who I always looked up to
Truth is I am so happy that I got the chance to meet you
Truth is I never dreamt that I would ever come this far
Truth is I'm here because of your effect on me not a wish upon a star
Truth is I appreciate you way more than I can ever show
Truth is some things are harder to put into words but this is a little start
Truth is all the words I write to you come from the bottom of my heart.
Truth is I'm happy that I can tell you exactly how I feel
Truth is people frequently ask God for someone just like you
Truth is to me it's a fantasy, like life is so unreal
Truth is you are original and you're good at what you do
Truth is people will do anything to have a friend just like you.

Find yourself

With every breath taken, with words never said,
Is one more emotion that you chose and you held.
With so little time being unsure of yourself is another
Precious moment wasted that could've been spent on something else.
With no hope left and all faith gone, you look in the mirror and wonder who you've become.
With strength and courage that's somewhere hidden inside,
You will find yourself again and you will no longer have to hide.

Red Carpet

I know you'll make it you've come this far
Just never forget the person who you are.
You've chased your dreams and they're coming true
Now the whole world is ready and waiting for you.
On your first red carpet walk of fame
I'll be one of the many fans on the sidelines
Screaming your name.
But before you go please promise this one thing.
Promise that you'll never forget about me.

Follow your Dreams

Where there's a cloud there's a dream
Where there's a mountain there's a world you've never seen.
Where there's sun, there is light that will all soon fade into the night.
Where there's a river somewhere there's an ocean that's bigger than you'll ever know;
But when you chase that cloud and climb that mountain the ocean will be yours to own.

L.O.V.E.D

Letting. Others. Vow. Eternal. Dedication.

My future your History

If the future brings us together
Or keeps us far apart
Just know that you will always have a special
Place in my heart.
The memory of when we first met,
And all of the laughs that we shared
Really helps me get past the days
That you are not here.

Golden Heart

You have a golden heart that you don't let people see.
You have the perfect arms that embrace me lovingly.
You have a gorgeous smile that can light up an entire room.
You have the ability to make people happy again
when they are feeling blue.
You have the magic touch to brighten my whole entire day.
The words you say mean everything and they will never fade away.
I have a special place waiting for you in my heart;
But the only problem is I haven't found you yet.

I'll wait

I'll never reject you,
always respect you,
but if you feel like I do
it's only because I'm trying to keep my heart
from being broken into two.
I'll hold on for now to something this special
to me even if you decide to let go.
But forever is just so far away so I'll wait for you
but you have to let me know.

Rescue Me

I'm not a damsel in distress or someone who needs to be saved
But at this moment in time I need for you to come and rescue me.
I cannot feel my heart for it is broken into two.
I do not know how I can heal it unless I am with you.
I cannot handle any more stress but it continues to follow me
But if you come to my rescue I can finally say that I am free.

Special Key

If I told you a secret would you share it with the world or
Would you keep it to yourself because I trusted that you could?
If I give you the key will you treat it with respect; use it if and only if
You are willing to commit. If I gave you my heart and told you to keep it in one,
Would you give it back whole or shatter it in tons?

One Love

In this life I think it's safe to say that finding love is not far away.
We search and search and we come to find that the one we
Have searched for is somewhere nearby.
You can always tell when this is the one when words can't describe
The moment you met. So do not give up when one breaks your heart; it's a
Matter of time when your one true love will come back.

Forever Yours

If you ever see me smile I picture that you're by my side.
If you ever see me crying please don't be the reason why.
If you feel like I am hurting please don't hesitate to ask.
If you really care about me please don't ask about my past.
The darkest moments are tucked away and I don't want to relive them.
But I still have a future and all I ask God is for a future with you in it.
If you ever walk away without telling me goodbye,
please find me again in the future and let me know the reason why.

Our song

Give me a beat I'll write you a song
that'll tell you how I feel.
I've got the chorus you take the verse
together we'll search for the perfect beat.
You take one octave I'll take it higher
we'll search for the harmony within.
In the last phrase I'll drop out and
I want you to tell me exactly how you feel.

Forever and Always

Your kiss made me weak
With one simple touch I could barely speak
Hearing the sound of your voice
Had me feeling like I didn't have a choice;
To be with you or without you
But I knew that I did.
I chose a path that benefited you
And left my heart broken in the end.
I got back up and stood up tall
Not yet recovering from the fall
The impact that you had on me
will forever live on in my memory.

I'll Be

I'll be the dream you always had if I could make you mine.
I'll be the wish you've always wished for and we can treasure this moment in time.
I'll be the girl you fantasize about and who is always on your mind.
I'll do my best to make you happy in hopes to never let you down.
On rainy days and stormy nights when nothing seems to shine;
I'll be the reason you wake up in the morning and say
I'm glad she's mine.

Three words Eight Letters

I have so much I need to say
Four phrases
Three words
Eight letters
each I'll lead the way.
Everyday my heart breaks a little more and more,
I need you in my life to be my one and only cure.
Hours pass day by day,
I miss you like crazy what else can I say.
I am sorry I'm not who you want me to be
but I know I should never apologize for just being me.
No matter what your feelings are now
or what you felt in the past, I want you to know
I love you and I will never take it back.

Dedicated to...

Best in me

I'm so happy to say that you are a part of my life
So I'll take the time now to thank all of you
Just right….

A.P., C.J., and J.J.

You were there for me beyond any doubt
You helped find the beauty within me inside and out.
Always knowing the right things to say
And putting the smile back on my face.
You talked me through all of my pain
Helped me understand that love wasn't a game.
When he tried to play with my heart you told me
He was the one who was missing out.
Thank you for helping me find the deeper side of myself
You helped bring out the best in me without any doubt.

Devon Aaron

I was so glad when you came into my life.
I can honestly say that you made my whole entire world shine bright.
You helped me open up my eyes now I'm making all of my dreams come alive.
You may not have known it at the time, but you showed me things that I would often hide.
Up till now I couldn't see that you were a blessing that God sent to me.
Although I'd disagree with what you seen
I see now that you've brought out the best in me.

Kurt Poole

You may have insulted me a little too much,
But the compliments you gave to me covered them up.
I know now that everything you said was true, and
I am so glad I took the time to listen to you.
You taught me not to look down on my flaws,
they're what makes me beautiful
So embrace them all.
You made me laugh and that was more than enough
to help me get past the days that were tough.
Even if you couldn't tell whether or not I was hurting,
every hug that you offered really did help with my healing.
I wanted to tell you know what that meant to me,
Thanks for being there blindly, bringing out the best in me.

Katie Harper

I want to thank you so much for always listening to me
And I will never forget the day that you stepped in to comfort me.
Somehow I felt that you could tell when things were on my mind
You talked to me when I cried even though I never gave you the reasons why.
Thank you for the shoulder that you lent to me and
Bringing out the best in me.

Ashley Johnson

I am so proud to say that you're my best friend
And my sister. I couldn't have asked God for anyone
Else that would make me feel so special.
Everything that we've been through when we were only kids
Made our relationship growing up stronger
Over the years.
Even now if we don't always see from eye to eye
We both know that we only have each other's best interest in mind.
Thank you for never turning your back on me.
I will always appreciate you for bringing out the best in me.

Mom

You are my supporter
You are everything I need
Without you I would not have become
the person who I've always wanted to be.
You taught me how to appreciate the finer things in life.
When I was unsure of myself you ensured me that
My future would shine so bright.
I know that something as simple as this will never be enough
To thank you
I love you so much and I wanted to say that you
Put the best in me.

End...

Words couldn't describe how I felt
Or how to thank you enough for helping me find myself.
So remember if you ever need a friend,
I will be there for you till the end.

Inspired by:

Live each day to the fullest- Angela Johnson

Find yourself- Ashley Johnson

Red Carpet, Truth is- Devon Aaron

Follow your dreams- Everyone who encouraged me to,

Encouraging everyone else to do the same.

Printed in the United States
By Bookmasters